skindancing

Susan Richardson

with illustrations by Pat Gregory

INDEPENDENT INNOVATIVE INTERNATIONAL

Published by Cinnamon Press
Meirion House,
Glan yr afon,
Tanygrisiau
Blaenau Ffestiniog,
Gwynedd, LL41 3SU
www.cinnamonpress.com

ISBN: 978-1-909077-63-8

Designed and typeset in Palatino by Cinnamon Press

Cover from original artwork 'skindancing' by Pat Gregory, © Pat Gregory

Printed in Poland
Cinnamon Press is represented in the UK by Inpress Ltd www.inpress-books.co.uk and in Wales by the Welsh Books Council www.cllc.org.uk

Acknowledgments

Thanks to the editors of the following anthologies and journals in which some of the poems in this collection first appeared: *Entanglements — New Ecopoetry* (Two Ravens Press); *Dark Mountain,* Issue 3; *Dark Mountain,* Issue 4; *For Rhino in a Shrinking World* (Poets Printery); *Furies — A Poetry Anthology of Women Warriors* (For Books' Sake); *Earthlines; Plumwood Mountain — An Australian Journal of Ecopoetry and Ecopoetics; The Journal of Wild Culture; Nature in Legend and Story; Not On Our Green Belt; Envoi; The Seventh Quarry; New Walk; The Learned Pig; Ouroboros Review; The Stare's Nest; Her Mark* (Woman Made Gallery, Chicago).

Audio versions of a number of the poems have also featured in several recent exhibitions — *Exile: A Living of Forest* at ONCA Gallery in Brighton and *Nocturne* at Fringe Arts Bath. Thanks so much to the curators.

Gratitude, too, to all the many human and non-human animals who've inspired me, over the past few years, to scratch this route through Hamelin.

And to Dad, whose long-ago, read-aloud bear stories were what got me started.

About the Author

Susan Richardson is a Wales-based poet, performer and educator, whose two previous collections, *Creatures of the Intertidal Zone* and *Where the Air is Rarefied*, themed around her own, and others', journeys through the increasingly fragile Arctic environment, are also published by Cinnamon Press. She is currently poet-in-residence with the Marine Conservation Society. Susan has performed at literary, environmental and science festivals throughout the UK, for organisations such as WWF and Friends of the Earth, on BBC 2, and at Universities both nationally and internationally. She has also been a regular performer on BBC Radio 4 while resident poet on Saturday Live.

For further information, please visit:
www.susanrichardsonwriter.co.uk

Contents

skindancing

Let my words be bright with animals
— from 'Prayer' by Joseph Bruchac

Let my verbs be studded with Glow Worms.
Let Painted Ladies flit from each vowel I sound.
Let my prose be overwritten with Purple Frogs.
Let Baboons moon at my proper nouns.
Let Flamingoes paddle in the shallows of my gossip.
Let Clownfish swim in memories' depths.
Let Satin Bower Birds use my blue language
to decorate their nests.
Let Bonobos get personal with my pronouns.
Let Impalas graze the great plain of my tongue.
Whenever I sing, from the roof of my mouth
let Orange Fruit Bats hang.
And at night, as darkness peaks,
let a Two-toed Sloth creep upside-down
through my mumbling canopy of sleep.
Let Wildebeest migrate with my yelling.
Let my softer speech be beached with Natterjack Toads.
Let Pygmy Hippos tinge my whispers.
Let my winter breath make Baiji-wraithes
and Dodo-ghosts.

as transformations go...

The White Doe

As transformations go,
this has no more daunt than the suddening
of blood and breasts. It's horizontal at its best—
belly hammocked between four legs
instead of back-trapped, compliant-wifing.

Though my hands have hooved,
they're now attuned to fungus-rub and moss.
My teeth are flossed heatherly,
I splursh through burns
and I've learned to ask the sun to fondle-flank
after twenty-one dark-cursed years.
Birch bark tonguing me.
Crossbills beaking pine seeds tweakily from cones.
Ground-smelling rowan, berrily with otterness.
Ear-twitch to a cracklish sound—
worker ants nest-mounding.
All such a gorgeous—
not even the flies round my side-head eyes
can undeer me now.

At last I can be forgettish—
no more bracelets, grammar, manners,
standard lamps, strip lights.
No more room-fug of stew
and my stale mother's breath.
No more lonelies and youfreaking.
No more curtains, shutters, blinds.

Instead, my hind-mind's ferned
with ancient memories of wolf
and the urge to neverstill.
Though the man I was meant to wed
turns hunter,
I will out-wood him.
For an unlife in the unlight
has taught me slinkness,
and how to happyeverafter
when I tellme tales.

We wore

hawks in our hair that year —
Harris hawks, who migrated
from marshes and mangroves
to frosted highlights and frizzy perms.
We loved them for mantling our blushes
and crooked teeth,
and for the way they preyed on the thesaurus
when we were lost for words.
Our classmates gasped in double French
as they swooped on Camus
or hovered, graceful as conjugation,
just above our desks.
Best of all, we got excused from games
when the netball bibs failed to stretch
over our heads.

Meanwhile, our mothers tutted,
feared futures deplumed
of proposals and proper jobs, pecked us
to deck ourselves in ra-ra skirts
and *Frankie Says* instead.

Only at exam-time did our hawks feel heavy,
adding to the weight of Hamlet quotes
and lateral moraine.
Come summer, they moulted osmosis, Napoleon,
and tore the square on the hypotenuse to shreds,
while we fed them live A-grades
and dreamed of boys
with squirrels round their necks.

We expected to wear them forever.
Till, one day, taking Polaroids for penfriends,
we waited for the image to form

and saw no hawks at all.

> In the very earliest time,
> when both people and animals lived on earth,
> a person could become an animal if he wanted to,
> and an animal could become a human being.
> Sometimes they were people
> and sometimes animals
> and there was no difference.
> — 'Magic Words' (after Nalunglaq)
> from *The Netsilik Eskimos* by Knud Rasmussen

If it wasn't for the chill
I still equate with getting naked.

If it wasn't for the way he fixates
on my hair — *Awesome colour,*
d'you henna it?

If it wasn't for the absurdity of skirts —
trailing, but failing to swish
like a tail.

If it wasn't for the yipping litters of words
I must birth and nurture daily.

If it wasn't for how my stealth
unnerves him —
Christ, you made me jump,
I didn't hear you come in.

If it wasn't that risotto's
no substitute for voles.

If it wasn't for having to scavenge
for apt emotions,
in bin bags crammed with irony
and scraps of shame.

If it wasn't for the tyranny
of being upright.

The full moon
was in Scorpio
and i was like okay
i'm ready to wake up
to my potential here,
manifest my
destiny, open
my third eye. So i
do a meditation, right,
and the message i
get is to sit
in siddhasana and
channel the cosmic energy
of the snake so i'm like
doing my kriya and
i'm *so* feeling it i'm
so connected the
snake's awakening
all the way up
my spine and
now i'm not
chanting i'm
hissing, right, and
my sacral chakra's
clearing and i look
down and omigod
my belly's covered
in *scales* and
i'm like
wow Siri Lakshmi
what have you
done here? Yogi
Rajpreet says
kundalini lets
you experience
infinity in the
finite so i haven't
got a clue how
long it lasted. I'm
totally cool
with it though and
first thing
tomorrow i'm
gonna go get
a snake tattoo.

Campervan's knackered again,
expelling repellent trails
of black smoke,
with none
of the grace
of my glisten.

Lock up your lettuce.
Cloche your hostas.
When I'm this mad,
I can't stop regressing.

If you're
French,
my revenge
will be
especially
slow.

born wrong-bodied
scorned bipedaling
mourned the closures
of mines and minds

sought cellars subways
cupboards under stairs
wore sunglasses in the dark

dug gardens graves
lonely holes
drove bulldozers
through the night

snouted out counselling
swallowed grubs of advice
tunnelled from self
to self for a year

then drugs for fur
for reduction of sight
to cultivate an appetite
for worms

then
the knife

under here
all is subtext
eruptions above
hide the secrets of subsex
right-bodyness of burrows
mud's velvet hug

I don't wanna talk about it, mate. Really don't wanna talk. Weirds me out every time I think of it.

But yeah, me and the lads were at the cricket. Edgbaston. In fancy dress 'cause that's tradition, innit, the Saturday of the Test. This year, we had a bit of a jungle theme going—Stu's a lion, I'm a tiger and there's elephants and crocodiles and shit. Anyhow, sun's blazing down, we've had a few beers, sodding South Africa's 430 for 2 and we're up on our feet, singing our lungs out—*Jimmy is our 'ero, na na na naaa*—to get behind the boys a bit...but suddenly Stu stops. I've taken my tiger head off and shoved it under the seat and Stu's gawping at me, got a look on him like I never seen before—*Mate*, he says, *Mate, listen to me. Your face is covered in fucking fur.* And South Africa hit another bastard boundary and everything else is just carrying on around me—*This wicket, there's bugger all in it for the bowlers...Enga-lund, Enga-lund, Enga-lund!*—and I'm standing there going *Nah, mate, you're winding me up* but he's told it like it is, and I'm gutted, absolutely gutted...

Like I said, though, I don't wanna talk about it.

It was the dodgy pasty I ate, that's all.

I'd just done the Waitrose shop and stopped off
at Wish Upon A Spa on my way to
lunching with The Girls. I'd booked Kaylee for
My Usual—but I'm assuming new
serum or toner was used, for as well
as the customary tingling, I felt
an unprecedented stiffening, which
evolved into the emergence of a
rather striking beak. My Eldest is, of
course, appalled. Blames me. Furious. Point-blank
refuses to talk. Bella, my Youngest,
is on her Gap Year—best not tell her What's
What, I suppose, while she's still in Chile
and Peru. My Middle One thoughtfully
informs me that I surely need Trauma
Therapy—but it's not like I've got AIDS,
for God's sake, or The Big C. I'd say it's
Just My Age—one more unforeseen symptom
to be forced to take on board. And let's be
blunt—at This Stage In Life, it gives one Quite
A Rush to induce a few heads to turn.
Not Hugh's though. I doubt he's even noticed.

Top Tips For Whipping That Irksome Work Stress!

Tip One: Recognise the Warning Signs!

Feeling on edge and angry—
my formic acid fantasy.
Months of disrupted sleep—
my marching dream.

Tip Two: Treat Yourself!

Ditch the lesson plans and marking.
Fill my bath to the brim with sugar.
Crawl in.

Tip Three: Surround Yourself With Supportive Friends and Colleagues!

Leave trails of my concerns for the colony to follow.

Wait for them to over-
lay the scent.
      chill
      a bit
      will
      you—
      you're
      such a
      stress-
      head
      all
      those
      long
      holidays—
      you
      teachers
      have
      got
      it
      made

<u>Tip Four: Remember—You Are More Than Just Your Job!</u>

Remember—I was always just my job.
Yet never calmer, from head
to metasoma.

Remember—now I must be
my own queen.

and no-one reads books on the train any more they're all on their i-whatnots and e-whatdoyoucallits and no-one wants to talk any more either but this chap opposite well I saw him rolling his eyes and snorting he looked fed up to the back teeth just like me when they gave some half-baked excuse for the train running late and I said bloomin' joke the trains we've got a poor bloomin' excuse for a transport system back when it was British Rail we all used to moan a bit but it was never this bad and they've put the fares up again and you don't get a seat half the time and he said oh I don't mind the squeeze or having to stand where I come from I'm used to it it's the delays that get me down and I said yes I know my daughter works on the continent and you get a lovely seat on the trains over there and they always run on time never late but here it's always leaves on the line or the wrong kind of snow or the driver doesn't turn up or there's an incident outside Swindon or the signals fail at Bristol Parkway and he nodded and snorted again bulky bloke he was too and no oil painting I can tell you so where you from then I said Africa he said and I said I didn't know there was much call for commuting over there oh yes he said not every day as such more like one big trip a couple of times a year oh I said well I bet you know all about travel hold-ups then over in Africa and he said no not at all never had to rely on trains we could please ourselves all of us leave whenever we wanted make our own way together under our own steam thousands of us there'd be and tell you the truth he'd lost me by this time but the girl sitting at the table next to him slip of a thing she was looked like a breath of wind could just pick her up and carry her off painting her nails too orange and black with funny white spots at the top strange way to paint your nails if you ask me and on the train of all places anyhow this girl smiled at him and he stared at her for a good deal longer than was necessary and then he said let me guess butterfly and she said got it in one monarch you?

When warbling to win me a mate
stopped feeling thrilling,
when trilling in willows and elms
felt only so-so,
I decided to try instead
to vie for top billing—
transform and perform
as the star of a West End show.

I'll sing sexy, I'll sing nice,
I'll sing Lloyd Webber and Rice,
I'll sing A Star is Born,
I'll sing A Chorus Line (at any time but dawn).

I'll sing jazz and snazzy beats,
I'll sing that ode to me by Keats.
Here I go again (Mamma Mia!)
I'll even do Cats (they're my biggest fear).

Ain't got no agent,
ain't had no break,
ain't been no understudy,
which is bloody hard to take.
Ain't smelt no greasepaint,
ain't had five-star reviews,
ain't never been the one
producers seem to choose.

But still—
I'll sing as Calamity Jane,
I'll dance and sing in the rain,
I'll sing as my lady so fair (oh yeah)
and I'll sing in Berkeley Square.

touchtrunk   better than handhold
                trunk suck water   tea no

            sad around mother gone   all of us around

remembers come like sounds far away

        sit no   who   want far away sit no sit no   water

better than handhold
                            water full suck   tea no

                sad around mother gone   all of us around
remembers come rumbles far far ago
        hot dust   who

            better than handhold   long long away   who

want   bed no   who   want   home

                        new one longtime carry

                    all of us around
                            touchtrunk   better than handhold

        hot dust   big trunksound long long away

where's newone   where's allofusaround

                                    where's

24

Phorusrhacidae

This is not a guillemot
bobbing in the froth of our dreams
or a mallard dabbling in shallow water
for our shoots and seeds.
This is not a jay storing our acorn-mistakes
for future gorging, or a great grey owl braced
      for the   twitch
of lemming beneath our snow.
          No. And this isn't a fossil:
scientists who hypothesise —
flightless...exceeded two metres in height —
should unfledge their computer models and edge
into the light, where a beak slashes open
the belly of sleep, rips
the flesh from our skittish pledges,
crushes smug bones and scythes
the scrub as it hunts
our mammal logic.
          Futile to assume we can outpace it.
Useless to play dead.
Too late to plead now it copulates
          with greed, exchanges
gifts of shifted blame
and squats on top of our world, coercing
it to   crack.

Chaíro

Brown Dog chases your angst up trees
and leaves it hissing at a distance, far
from the satin cushion of your heart.

Brown Dog's glee-shaped bark
makes the panic-rabbits scatter.

Brown Dog attacks
the postman of despair, tears up
his sack of final demands, snatches
        from mid-air
your frisbees of fear.

Brown Dog never appears, eyes aglow,
at crossroads in the dark,
for each night he's pawing the sun, forcing
it to come out tomorrow.
Brown Dog shakes   grey   clouds
till they display their silver lining, chews up
your kitbag of troubles,
sinks his teeth into rubbery grief
to release the squealing.

Brown Dog follows your trail, yanks
you from the stinking dumps you're down in.
His tail whips up
        wind   in the doldrums;
his tongue-bunting makes even Churchill grin.

Brown Dog sniffs your body-length
then pisses stars and glitter —

       This is my joyspace!   *This!*   *This!*   *This!*

Animals are 'good to think [with]'
— Claude Lévi-Strauss

To be in two minds, think amoeba. To sell
tea, think chimp. To build your own beak,
think owl. To lick jowls and vomit logic,
think wolf. To be insulted, think cow. To
turn your voice inside-out, think crow.
To balance the earth on your back, think
turtle. To force reason to ingest itself,
think sea squirt. To birth the first person,
think raven. To paint yourself into a cave,
think stag. To drag silk scarves from a
hat, think coyote. To sell toilet rolls, think
dog. To wear your bones on your sleeve,
think crab. To sell alco-fizz, think deer.
To sell beer, think bear. To wagspeak,
think dog. To de-rib, think gnat. To
revertebrate, think bat. To chemchat,
think ant. To sell mints, think fox. To toss
your testicles over your shoulder, think
raccoon. To be insulted, think pig. To sell
paint, think dog. To gaze with disdain
on naked philosophy, think cat. To taste
leaves with your feet, think butterfly.
To sell sweet underarms, think lynx.
To hatch sunyolk and skywhite, think
duck. To cup fireballs with your tongue,
think fox. To listen with your legs, think
spider. To ditch hypothesis, think hippo.
To insist it isn't possible, think bat. To
drift to earth in a radiant cradle, think
bear. To sell shoes, think puma. To forfeit
four feet, think octopus. To glowtalk,
think firefly. To sell insurance, think dog.
To be insulted, think shrew. To dive for
silt and make mountains, think muskrat.
To sell cars, think mustang. To sell cars,
think panda. To sell cars, think jaguar.
To sell cars, think beetle. To get drunk,
think skunk. To bask on a rock though
you don't know it as such, think skink.

Der Löwenmensch

Lion Man is carved from a mammoth tusk.
The man who carves him is excused from other tasks
like predating reindeer, making scrapers and spears.

> *Lion Man is carved with a flint tool from a mammoth tusk.*
> *The woman who carves him continues*
> *her usual tasks of garnering tubers and herbs,*
> *and suckling young.*

Lion Man is carved to enable the shaman to effect
his connection with the spirit of lion, to solicit
an auspicious hunt.

> *Lion Man sleeps myth-deep in a hundred pieces.*
> *As world war roars, the men who uncover him*
> *scramble to cache their prey.*

Lion Man half-stands in half-light under glass.
The woman who beholds Lion Man
takes notes on her phone, reads the exhibition text, forgets
to listen to the fur rise along the length of her neck.

> *Lion Man is carved maneless*
> *while in the ivory cave lie the remains*
> *of Lion Man's breasts.*

The casting of Lion Man far from the hearth
shows how Lion Clan outgrows its name.

> *Lion Man is carved to enable the shaman to effect*
> *her transformation into lioness.*

Lion Man sleeps dread-deep,
carved for a child curled under furs
to curb fears of shapes beyond the fire.

> *Lion Man's curator never wearies*
> *of his theories of totemic import, the Pleistocene polemic*
> *he imparts to his myriad visitors.*

The man who repairs Lion Man
calls him Bear Man and Man With No Face.

Lion Man is carved by a member of the lion man race,
descendent of ur-Lion Man, world creator.

Lion Man's curator snarls
at her pages of visitor data, blames
poor footfall on Lion Man
for being incomplete.

Lion Man half-stands in half-dark under glass.
The man who beholds Lion Man salivates,
smells each successive age of ice and heat.

Lion Man sleeps happiness-deep,
carved to make play with the first wolf-dog.

The placing of Lion Man far from the hearth,
away from the everyday,
makes plain his sacred status.

Lion Man sleeps forty millennia-deep and wakes
speaking German –
in Ulm um Ulm und um Ulm herum.

Lion Man is carved from a cave using a mammoth tusk.
Lion Man sleeps in forty thousand mythical pieces.
The man who's predated by a reindeer
tells Lion Man to fill in his own blanks.

Awen

quicker than an ear's fear-prick
quicker than instinct quicker
than the fist of a jill on jack than
roads slicing through meadows and
mowers through leverets so quick
it's tea-time tomorrow next week
saprise leafdrop cropspray herbwilt
so quick decades have died since i sipped
that soup of ceridwen and (yes i guess
it sounds strange but i've outrun
march and feel perfectly sane) i'm so quick
i've reached the next geological age
(an unaesoped place—no parables,
lakes or arable land) so quick i spill
my knowledge-stock and
must double-back to retrieve it so quick
i catch up with a future me—
shocked   i stop
to river-watch
from a form beneath this tree
and wait for the time
when we and she must coincide
and lungpump's swapped for gills

Though soon my flesh will feel air's caress
   From all sides,
This water is way more persuasive—
My scales can't escape
The hurble and blursh of its purpose.
And as it immerses me in my pre-prehistory,
Not for one plish does it let me forget
That I failed to outpace her
And must aim now to outpatience her instead.

No need to shoal breamily or leap
For the place where I was born, to spawn.
I'll just wait here, unseen,
Chubbing under the cover of overhanging trees
And even when the distance between us
Seems fin-thin, I will linger, staid as Sunday.

Will she stay, canined, on the brink?
Will a bitterling-flicker in her mind
Prick her to leave?
If she peers in, will she think
Her splushy reflection is me?
Or will she glimpse her gudgeon grudges,
Bottom-feeding,
Nudging her to plunge in?

this learning to us has been so rushed
making chatter patterns
duskly hundred-neighbour natter
flap overlap swiftswitch cloudspace
swirl

but now us is a one-us
a glory-us for nourish the usness
for ussing us-selves from loss-land
food-short and fright

when she comes
as us knows she must
us shall stun her with airstunt
with an us-shunt of sky
just as sky realigns the us

though she'll try to un-us
she'll cuss our dizzy-dazzle
us-gloss of flight

us loves to live thus
usly

am single syllable
synonym for wisdom
still-life with stillness

minding own is-ness
witness to henpeck and windwhim—
no other means to move

yet old knowing of swim
speed   flight
plus all future shift and insight
are compressed within
in plumule and radicle

didn't plan to unanimal—
feared her talons loomed
so swooped inside
then ungenetically modified

now crash course in chaff
adrenaline-lack
too zen for active flock or shoal

no more goals of flee
hide hope she'll bore
daze with sleight of wing

instead embrace this barnfloor fate
cultivate a durum state of mind
meditate on swish of scythe

imitate silence

...thoughts were like animals in the forest
— Carl Jung

There were always scores of grey squirrels,
forcing the reds north, corkscrewing
round trunks. And there were often
great spotted woodpeckers, persistently drilling.
He kept the dormice hidden,
huddled in leaf litter, tucked among roots,
but the rutting fallow buck—
unbracketing fungi as antlers rubbed bark—
he could never conceal.

Some nights, a tawny owl yanked him from sleep,
and dangled his soul, like a bank vole, from its claws,
while pipistrelles gorged on his mothy dreams.
And once, he was roused
by a sounder of wild boars, uprooting
his bluebell caution.

Part of his mind, it's true,
was a conifer plantation for commercial use,
that fewer creatures than usual frequented.
And yes, he could have done with some dryads
and talking bears, an outcast child who'd soon transform,
a Robin Hood. Yet at its best,
his head was an Atlantic oakwood, mossy
with possibles, otters rippling
through burns, surging
with ferns and returning beavers.

Now, though,
his ancient oaks are felled.
His badgers culled.
His redpolls silent.
As his ash dies back,
there's even a scheme
for selling off
his forest's remains.

The Entomologist's Dream

after a painting by Edmund Dulac

We only meant to rearrange
ourselves, claim the wrong Latin names, swap
boxes, but when we first escaped
and saw him squirm against the wall,
we were gripped
         by the urge
    to swarm,
        to form a tizz
  of unhinges, a blur
    of turning pages of the most disturbing
stages of his life,
a blizz of accusing
           eyespot-gazes.

No more killing jar twitch,
thorax pin, chitin-rip,
post-chrysalis crucifixion.

For we are the stutters   in his chest,
    his   guilt   flits and ego   flutters,
we are his midnightly mutters — the words
he should have uttered fifty years ago.
We're the flustered breath of his young lover
(when she looked upon his face,
he forsook her for ever).

We mean this dream to be a wing —
thin enough for him to wake,
but only so we can make it beat
again and
again and
again.

**You'll never become a rhinoceros, really you won't…
you haven't got the vocation**
— from *Rhinocéros* by Eugène Ionesco

There comes a day when making donations
and signing petitions isn't enough,
when braver decisions are needed.
So you practise detachment
from your knees,
trample the lunchtime prattle of fat loss
and anti-wrinkle creams.
You commit to omitting to moisturise,
will your skin to thicken,
thrill to fashion callouses and warts.

When the first horn forms, it triggers
second thoughts, till you use it to gore
your twinges of caution.
From raw veg and fruit, you move
to woody shrubs and thorns,
snort through weeks
of stomach cramps and wind.
But the wallowing's a breeze,
and the shift to horizontal's eased
by your umpteen years of yoga.

Next to varied breathing speeds
and scent-marking middens of dung,
texting seems so naive. In fact,
if you still had fingers and thumbs
you'd just use them to pinch yourself,
for you've done what none
can believe. And while the strain of raising
your head has led
to chronic pain in your neck,
your brain hums with infrasonic success.

As you roam your home range,
oxpeckers divest you of ticks
and outmoded emotions,
though you insist they must not strip you
of awareness
of your rare, endangered state.

Thylacine

i was per-
haps. i am may-
be. Was nearly now, al-
most then. Ex-
tant, ex-
tinct, ~~just visiting~~, dithering
with existence. Am
listed as critical. Was
history. Soon rumoured.
i am virtually ~~non- un-~~ on
the brink of unique,
(in)conceivably, (un)feasibly
a ~~one-, two-~~, none-off.
Am RIP. Yet just as i re-
ceive a cairn of commemoration
i glimpse myself from the cor-
ner of my eye and

it was about ten metres away when I first
noticed it. Sun was going down and I was stuffed after walking all
day so I was waiting by the stream for Jase to put up the tent and
make a fire and whatever the fuck else he does when he says it's
time to camp. Thought it was a dog at first—it was about the size
of Jase's sister's Lab, the one that flobs all over you, kind of pale
like a Labrador too, but then I saw the stripes, and its body looked
weird—like heaps longer than it should've been. I was too freaked
to move, just sat there, couldn't breathe, couldn't even reach in my
shorts for my phone. And just when I'm thinking I'm so going to
pass out here, it turns round and disappears into the bush. And
soon as it's gone, Jase comes over—took his fucking time—and
says *I've got the fire going, Soph. This place is unreal!...Aw, what's up?*
You look like you've seen a

~~dog-~~ wolf-headed,
~~zebra-~~ tiger-rumped.
i have bygonned
my image
on the rock. They called me
coorina, loarinna,
~~chimerical miracle~~.
i am ~~thresh-~~ flesh-
holding, solid as persecution,
dwelling in the realm

of (im)possibility where
there are fewer eucalypts
than there ever used to be.
Was i a ~~clever~~ fake? The proof
is (in)conclusive. My
marsupial pouch holds
only fables now—
the bandicoot i toss
to see which way it lands,
stars miraging
the loss of my ~~before~~
after. Yet as i dis-
locate my jaw
with a ~~phantom yawn~~ a scream,
i dream clean pawmarks
in the mud and

mate, I couldn't believe
my eyes. It was gone midnight, I'd skulled a few beers and
was driving home over the Burrenbidgee. Parked by the bridge
and got a pretty good squiz—it was standing there, ears up,
tail out stiff like the tail of a roo—and then I thought I'd hop
out the van and get a bit closer. Mate, if I'd only had the three-
oh-eight Winchester with me—guys spend years out in the
bush trying to bag one of these bastards. Tried to film it on my
phone before it shot through, but it was too shit-dark to see, so
I grabbed my torch from the van and hunted round for a while
and found what I reckon was a paw print. Soon as I got home,
I googled it and, mate, I was

~~right~~ wrong,
(un)imaginable, (barely)
credible, a twilit wishful
think delivered
by the (un)conscious mind.
Whistle me up, make me ~~limbo~~
~~liminal~~ (in)visible,
see what you ~~expect~~
~~hope~~ grope to see. Am
psychopomp, tulpa,
(preter)natural personal guide.
Was a figment of my
~~hallucination~~.
(Not even) quasi-

He kept

his hippo under the stairs, snuggled
between the Hoover and Ewbank,
encouraged it to wallow
in old duffels and cagoules.

His wife immersed its bellows and grunts
in Terry Wogan and Jimmy Young,
insisted on no visitors, scrubbed
the Formica of semblances of mud.

His son, too, refused its existence,
except, each Christmas,
when fetching Ludo or Buckaroo,
he'd roar at the squashed box.

In time, his wife implied her home
was too small for megafauna—
what about my new Dyson?—
so he shifted his hippo to the shed.

There, it leaked rust, and slept,
head wedged in the yawn
of the wheelbarrow,
rump uplifting the bench.

Now, since his wife's demise,
his son long-distance-calls each month,
urges him *to get shot of stuff
while you're still fit enough.*

Side by side with his hippo,
watching cricket on Sky, he grins.
For he's learnt, when submerged, to close
both nostrils and ears, and knows

that the moment he decides,
jaws stretched wide enough can engulf
a whole house and its contents.
An entire life.

The Preseli Ridge

is a Basset's back today, peat patching
through snow, like morning through
a dream. From iron age fort to stone circle to

spotted dolerite crags, she's trekked
the Neolithic track, to peak
at Foel Cwmcerwyn, where the gap between her

and history, history and myth, is mist-thin,
the air still as a secret to let the past in
without buffeting. A Labrador sun tongues the slopes

that sprawl towards the coast, slobbers
on conifers and a distant, listless tractor.
She's seen no other walkers,

no horses, buzzards, sheep,
yet feels sure the Twrch Trwyth,
the king cursed into the form of a boar, is here.

Hoarding the scissors and comb between his ears,
he's quit scuffling with Arthur,
snurfles at the trig point's base, shits cromlechs.

And look—he's hoofing a peat-pool's frozen surface,
rooting for proof of the wildwood,
bristles stiff, nostrils steaming.

She expels a bluestone breath,
icing the hair that strands from her fleece hat.
Soon the ridge will moult its snow coat

and begin to itch with sheep again,
while the lower slopes will be gorsing into bloom.
Wriggling chilled toes, she muses

that these thoughts of spring
seem so implausible, then chooses to zig-
zag downhill, pursued by what may

or may not be her long lilac shadow.

The Pen is Mightier

What seemed like a lover's tongue between my toes
was the forming of extra skin.
What my spine believed were prickles of unease
were the birth-hurts of feathers.
The words I found to shout and curse
hardened into a beak,
while the flex of my stretched neck almost choked me.

So now you've got the daughter you desired.
Bride-white. Pond-perfect.
And, aside from this ridiculous hiss,
no ability to vocalise.

But listen, mother—
when I appear to be gliding
or serenely preening, I will shrug
your fluffed-up gloats off my back
and plunge my head
                deep underwater.
I will see what you don't see, tease out
the tangles in the sub-aquatic weeds.

And when I emerge,
I'll learn to run on the surface, unfold
        my wing-cloak,
                        rise.
Watch me migrate
to the blank page of the tundra,
fill my bill with indelible sky   and begin

to write.

Lost in Llandudoch

The merfolk have never developed a written language. However, an early twentieth century mermaid, who successfully straddled the human- and mer-worlds of West Wales for many years, was persuaded to write down the tale of Flosha and Pergrin, transcribing, to the best of her ability, the oceanic whooshes and swooshes of her own language into the Roman alphabet she'd been taught.

The poem has since been rendered into both English and Welsh by a succession of different translators. This latest English version, produced in consultation with a renowned anthropoichthylogist, reflects an intimacy with the merfolk's vast, yet eminently precise, vocabulary of marine-related terms. Although the new translator remains faithful to the structure of the original (approximating, it is believed, a seven-wave pattern), he has essentially offered a liberal, rather than literal, interlingual rendition of the mermaid's words.

The mermaid's transcription appears here alongside the English translation for the first time.

Sleesh Flosha

Blesh yosh ush throopsa
blip Flosha shripsa
scosh lesh swisashi
slish mi, hoff mof Pergrin loth,
swishamassi,
blip lethmoffal,
stashi sosh mip lippla.

Sloll mof offrish flashla,
Flosha swol blip fleesh
boffle scosh fessishgresha
Flosha swos blishiswis thrisha
closhi swush
blip ploffle blip throosh dishla
blip Flosha swos molla.

Crishta mof solsha lishi
flissi sooshmisha plashla
lishta sosh blish, flishta sosh
ish wosh—*Plis flis flosh lishta, crish
slish flis sos throopsa blip pollsi
ploffta lisha flis.*
Blip sosh scoshi dishla, Pergrin sosh mishta.

Jeeshswoshla. Tishi yoshlish
pleffi floff moosh blip mooshi mip fashta,
slishi losh, throopsa shisha.
Ush Flosha sish looshlashie—
sish saswosh, stoshta
blip slessi, blip closhi fassish
mishla, crish osh pollisha.

Slish Pergrin sosh liff lipplesh
Flosha loshta sosh sooshtaflosh—
*Croshti swista. Croshti lishstasha.
Gloosa. Closhlasha.*
Slish stasha lalmoosh mas
motsa fliflif sosh blof
blip scolush shlif.

Ush Pergrin swos Flosha bloshtol
blip lollta bishta
cloosh swoshta blip lofflesha slish
soosha mi losh mip swoshloosha.
Flosha plisha flof sleeshi
ull sosh hallisha soosh.
Blip floff mosh ussalasha.

Lost in Llandudoch

It was moon of the stillsea
and she was kelping
in the lea of the pleated cliffs
when he, the one they called Pergrin,
billowing with herring-success
and happily unchapelled,
threw over her his extra net.

As they sailed for the mouth of the estuary,
she thrashed and wailed,
for in his longswimaway home,
she knew she'd be made to wear fullskin
instead of half scales
and knees and thighs in place of tail,
and she knew she'd be forced to part them.

Not till they crossed the sandbar
did a sparkling merthought surf
to the shore of her despair, urging her
to speak—*If you release me, I promise
that when you're at sea and I divine a storm,
I will always arrive to warn you.*
And with this pledge forevered in brine, Pergrin set her free.

Many tides turned. Come ficklemoon,
every village man and boy was in his ketch, catching fish,
believing the sea was soundsleeping.
Yet she sensed it was just pretending—
sensed from cloudspeak, from the prattle of pebbles
and shells—and had already swum
to the pupping beach, to coax the newborns to retreat.

Now, as soon as her eyes netted Pergrin,
she kept to her merword—*Beware
the shifting wind. Beware the switch
from green to grey.
Boat yourself home. Don't linger.*
When the other men heard, their laughter slammed
against her and broke in a spray of scorn.

But Pergrin knew she spoke true,
and uprivered with speed,
past grounded grebes and otters doing shelter-seek,
till he reached the refuge of his dwelling.
She dived deeper than the years of this tale
to her harbour of merness.
And the village unbelievers never returned.

Humanimal

Adlet

Measures his years in sevens.
Questions the sense in chasing
sticks. His neck is contested
territory—sometimes garbed
in a club tie, sometimes in
collar and disc. Overthinks
sniffing. Quits licking for Lent.

Bunzel

The Bunzel's love-shuffle starts on museum steps,
face freckled with Mohn,
fur flecked with Zimt. Even when he
        trips,
he still   hinks   at her side,
to meufel in the woods by the Kipferl-moon
at Schnarch-time.

Cernunnos

Likes spiking receipts; open-topped convertibles; cardis and
shirts. Likes inviting jays and grey squirrels
to perch. Hates Scottish estates; being draped
in coats, dogs' leads, bird feeders, baubles—
dreads Christmas. Wants his head etched on
a cauldron. Longs to roar on Exmoor
in autumn. Instead, edges sideways through doors.

Dog-headed Man

Won't stop licking till given
liver treats. Drops to hands and
knees to read the streets through his
nose. Wears kipper ties—there's so
much more to chew. Chases cats!
Sticks! Leaves! Chases cars! Gulls! Tail!
Measures the length of alone.

Ensorceleur des Trois-Frères

He waits cave-deep,
cet être mi-animal mi-homme,
he waits cave-deep.
Paints mammoths on our wall of sleep,
paints bison, woolly rhinos. Comme
un mystère, ce rêve nous consomme.
He waits cave-deep.

Fuglø, Edward
(Birds in Suits)

Gannet's
on i-dive.
Murre downloads migration
app. Fulmar spits oil
at online avatars.
Puffin's tweeting
#nuffin

Gunbim

In Kakadu did Gagudju
a painting of an emu make,
with human torso and a few
huge feathers. One more portrait too:
part-man and part-tree snake.
In time, this reptile came alive,
unmammalled by the long monsoon—

Heqet

Diet: tongue-flicks to catch flies, mosquitoes, moths,
passing thoughts, the current mood.
Habitat: fashions her own lily pad.
Behaviour: helps herself across the road.
Reproduction: refuses the hotch-potch
of suitors itching to prove she was the victim
of a botched kiss.

Iawll

The iawll is a stroke of athrylith.
A half-gwyllt half-afanc which builds half
the argaeau, fells hanner
the coed, irks half a ffermwr, needs a half-
ymgynghori taking hanner
the time, and has the ymenydd to lead
a full reintroduction campaign.

Jüngster Sohn

Blames his sister for not finishing his shirt.
Blames the witch for her anserine curse.
Blames his mother for not birthing him first.
Blames the moon for being distant from the earth.
Plucks feathers from his wing till it hurts.
Yearns to break girls' arms.
And worse.

Kitsune

Her skirt billows like thunderclouds. She's glaring as she
licks chicken from her fingers on the corner of Vulpes
Street, daring muggers, nuns, her mother, to discover
what's underneath.

dawn-red sun—
pavement brushed
by her caudate shadow

Liu Xue
(We Are the World)

When she got sick
of being told to eat,
she chickened her legs,
unthickened her feet.
Hollowing bones
just needs self-control and oh
it feels almost perfect.

This'll teach her to nag
(Tim, join a gym.
Quit bingeing on bread.
You really should shed sixty pounds.)
Gloriously walrus
from the torso
down.

Monkey Bride

To groom, to cherish.
To have and to hold.
To beget the best
of both primates.
Arched feet
and opposable
toes.

Nüwa

She's slith and swag,
rept and mamm
flexib yet inelast.
She succ
to her own temptation
she crea,
        then unmak.

Onocentaur

Listen up. I didn't misuse unction
like Lucius craving some avian shape.
Nor is this a slip-on skin whose function
is to shit gold to help a girl escape
her husband-father. And unlike that jape
of Puck's—fairy queen, love juice in each eye—
I'm unchangeable. Half-ass till I die.

Piccinini, Patricia
(The Long Awaited)

The ever after that's never seen—
sea sponge breasts,
hair like dried thongweed,
flaking scales shorn of their sheen.
Yet she's happy as the deep,
even when wrinkling
            into sleep mid-

Quappen

Quite why the quappen won't quit laughing is
Unknown. He chuckles
As he crunches the last drumstick, as he
Pilfers pork scratchings in the
Pub. He guffaws when punches are thrown,
Even roars when he plunges into love—but
Never lets her in on the joke.

Ryder, Sophie
(The Lady-Hare)

*She's like so weird. Totes bizarro. Yeah, have you ever met
anyone else who looks as freaky-deak as she does? Bet
she owns a buttload of broomsticks! Yeah, and a skanky pet
black cat. Can see she's not getting any action!* Meanwhile,
eyes unblurred by tears, she's curled in tall grass, half-moons a smile,
twirls the length of one furred ear round her finger. Their habit
of branding her thus hurts not; the gibe she fears is rabbit.

Sphinx

Who eats by setting cryptic quizzes?
Who riddles with wildebeest,
brainteases buffalo,
gives number puzzles to gazelles?
Who plays sudokudu?
Who says *Three guesses!*
Wrong! Wrong! Wrong! Let us prey!

Thoth

Handwrite or laptop? My dear,
this might surprise you. Neither.
Using the beak works best for me.
Suffused with estuary light.
Kindled by the miracle of crustaceans.
Mining an exclusive route to the sumptuous ooze
of the subconscious.

Unsettled Dogs
(Sam Jinks)

Today, she's the first to wake. His snout furrowing the pillow. Last night's field mouse on his scuttling breath. The scruff of his neck where fur begins to give way to the autocracy of skin. She clamps shut her eyes as red-jacketed doubts crowd in.

crack
in the curtains
the vulpine sun

Vallinas, Miguel
(Second Skins)

Too. Much. Neck.
Takes me days to unknot its length
when I'm hot-desking.
Could mark a question.
Hook a sheep.
A heavy curtain.
That lush vulture off the bus.

Whitehead, Simon
(Loup 2)

She found her wolf voice in the city,
in the alpha dark of Brandon Hill.
   owooooo   owooooo   owoooooooooooooooo
In the answering pack, she heard a siren,
hens on staggering heels, the falter
of a clock running out
                       of time

Xenotransplant

and each night this heart propels you to the woods
where all at once you're a-grunt on your knees and
then you're nosing earth and you dig with ungloved
hands for this heart has made you learn the democracy
of mud and the lumps you root up are the texture of
guilt and quite against your will you must consume
them for the blood that this heart pumps is not its own

Youwarkee

Youwere warned about Icarus and Cumulonimbus.
Youwere bored by Peregrine Awareness.
Youwhinged about the relevance
of the History of Zeppelins.
Youwrote a flimsy essay on Consistency of Air.
Youwalked from all gym sessions called
Strengthening Yourwings.

Zoo Portraits
(Yago Partel)

wags school for the gabba   grabs
            a   snooze as the game gets underway   dozes
through   the   first innings   zizzes
                all afternoon   misses
        the next   six   wickets   wakes
            for his eucalypt fix
                            at close of play

Pwll y Wrach

Yes, I confess I was ejected
from those woods where I spelled
girls into deer and men into bears,
and yes, I veered west, hurdled one sea,
then wester yet to this opposite
              of woods,
where kittiwakes crest knucklebone crags
and heckle the land-bound.

See those cliffs? They're not Ordovician.
All the buckles
              and rucks, the rifts
and the folds, are mine.
I shoulder-shunted   the sandstones and shales,
licked out that cwm,
filled it with spit, then blasted
a pit with just one exhale,
where lichen and froth, shingle and salt,
can mingle. No, it's not geological,
this place where I still aim to save
the frustrated from their fate.

Take you, for instance.
I can smell that you're walking to escape—
yet you could go so much further
than the path's death at Amroth.
Come. Don't let your resolve flit
from squill to thrift like a Burnet moth.
My draughts are seasonal—
today, I give you stitchwort and sheepsbit.
Drink, and they'll trigger a shift
into guillemot or shag—seabirds are my specialty—
while two moons on,
swigging knapweed and betony will release you
              into seal.
You could even join my coven of slugs,
each one fat as a capstone.

I also offer unction.
Dump your rucksack. Roll your shoulders.
Feel me rub forth
              a choughful of wings.

If a lion could speak, we could not understand him
— Ludwig Wittgenstein

1.

If a lion could speak,
we'd hear how Kruger has flattened his vowels,
how Longleat's left him with a lisp,
how he's zoo-mute,
and how his tamer wields a whip
then delves between his jaws
to extract the stammer.

If a lion could speak,
we'd correct his grammar,
purge his syntactical savannah
of herds of double negatives,
then wince if he ripped
apart just one infinitive.

If a lion could speak
he'd sphinx-talk about the thorn in his paw,
how MGM lip-synced his roar
and how Albert gave him heartburn for weeks.

If a lion could speak,
we may deign to reply,
though very loud and slow,
like a lion's really a scarecrow in disguise.

If a lion could speak,
we'd insist he use English
but he'd cleave to Lionese.
The few of us who'd learnt Leopard
might grasp the lack of past and future tense,
while the rest would be baffled,
more concerned to learn
how to order a beer in Giraffe.

If a lion could speak,
we'd tire of his whinges of wardrobes and witches,
of how Richard filched his heart
and how his rampant act on flags
has knackered his hips.
In time, we'd surely ignore him,
drawn to the wit of warthogs,
and antelope banter instead.

If a lion could speak, he'd say *Take a degree*
in my language of strangling ungulates
and wrangling with vultures for the meat.
Then we'll talk.

2.

Wardrobes lack wit.
Warthogs insist on the use of a disguise.
We'd whip the rampant scarecrow if we could,
then, flattened, he'd rest with the lion he'd just filched.
For if his savannah-heart could grasp a lion's paw
who'd then speak of a grammar?

In the past, a baffled Albert gave the flags
a degree of order, while in future,
he could act like a giraffe.
How slow and how correct and how very English.

We'll speak to more ungulates
and wince with the vultures.
Kruger has a language of negatives but, in time,
his mute lion-hips could learn to talk.

How about a lion? Might a lion say how?
Witches would double-take if one really knackered lion
could ignore his thorn and tire of his infinitive.
We'd speak of his meat and we'd speak
of strangling him instead—him! him!

If ripped Richard has a Lionese lisp in his beer,
he'd cleave to his syntactical antelope for weeks.
How tense. How could he!

Vowels apart, surely we'd purge the lion
of his heartburn if lip-synced wrangling
between Longleat's jaws could be concerned.
Though tamer, his leopard delves
in his stammer and wields a roar.

If few reply to a left lion extract
and if herds learnt a loud sphinx of whinges
then how may my if-zoo deign to talk?

Speak, speak, speak—
we'd hear his MGM banter.
He's drawn to us—and how.

3.

I, alone. Cold. Bleak.
Wed her now. Nougat is fattened with owls—
so wrong. Pete's laughing—it's Alice
(oh, she's too cute!)
Anne's cow is famous—fields unzip
themselves, as green as yours.
Go—unpack this summer.

In an iron hood, creak—
bleed, infect sick grandmas.
Urgent, impractical caravans
of words have troubled relatives.
Head winds have been tipped
to start. Trust cunning primitives.

Misaligned woods—specks,
seeds, lynx, hawks are out, reborn of this whore-
house. Energy in whips sinks this sore
land. Now all hurt paving can't learn to shriek.

Is our crying good? Weak
tea, they claim, could repel
those scary-sounding hose-
pipes. Our crying's merely a shadow in these eyes.

Whiffy loins. Cod-piece.
Please desist. Refusing swish
butties, we got Chinese.
A blue office would spurn Leonard's
tights. Clasp a slack oaf, blast a few chairs, then
smile. At best, Ruby's raffles
are upturned, so burn
now too, border on fear of bar graphs.

Ivy lines old cheeks.
Weeds spiral in spring's onward probe. Banned wishes
have now stitched up rich wizards
around this lamp and baton. Flans
as lacquered as ships
win bindweed. Poorly pigs snore in
dawn's other pit. If bored dogs
stand on the slope, panda skin's red.

With a fine food geek, we may make a green pea
on rye sandwich. If handling young shallots,
add sand. Bring six sculptured forks, then eat
ten peeled stalks.

4.

rrrrrraaaaaw
raarrghgh [   ]
hffngh hffnggh hffngggh
rraaw rraaw rraagh
rraaaw [   ] raaaaghgh
rrgh rrgh rrrghhhh

rrrrrrraaaaaw
hffn hffngh rraaa hffn hffn hffn
[   ]
rwaaaarrw   rwaa   rwarrw
hff rrrr rrrr rrrr hraaaa
rraaaaghhh

rrrrrrraaaaaw
raaaaaaooowwrrrrrr [   ]
aaaarr aarr aaaaarrrr

rrrrrrraaaaaw
rrr rrr rrrrrr
hff hffngggh

rrrrrrraaaaaw
grrauuuw
rrrraaaaaaawwwr raaaaaawr
hfffnghgggh hff [   ]
rrgh rrgh rrgh rrrrrghghgh

rrrrrrraaaaaw
[   ]

rrrrrrraaaaaw
aaaaaoowrr aaaaawr aaaaaaaaoooooowrrrrrrrrrr

A Note on the Lionese Translation

For those less than familiar with Lionese, it will come as a surprise to see that Emeritus Professor Ross Sorenson's translation of the poem is significantly shorter than the English original. This is principally due to the fact that many of the concepts expressed in the poem are outside the realm of lions' experience and therefore have no direct Lionese equivalent; square brackets within the text indicate sections for which there is not even a distant approximation. In addition, some of the nuances of the translation are, of necessity, based on assumption[1], albeit assumption gleaned from Professor Sorenson's lifelong field research—studying, transcribing and translating the language of lions in every practicable context, from pre-hunt to post-coitus.

In addition to having no past or future tenses, Lionese has no passive voice and no conditional. It employs a surprisingly wide vocabulary[2] and there is manifest evidence of leonine self-awareness, as demonstrated by the use of both the first person singular[3] and first person plural[4] pronouns.

Although other languages in the Big Cats family, including Leopard and Jaguar, are notable for their frequent utilisation of the roar, the lion's is by far the most complex, 'arguably conveying more meaning, layers and intent than a Shakespearian soliloquy'[5]. Sixty-three different Lionese dialects have been identified by Professor Sorenson and although the lexicon of this poem approximates standard Lionese, it also bears some characteristics of the dialect of the Ngonyama pride of South Africa's Eastern Cape[6].

As for the current and future status of Lionese, the language is, at present, classified as vulnerable due to substantial population decline[7]; however, unlike certain other languages, such as Quagga and Pyrenean Ibex, it is unlikely to fall out of use in the foreseeable future. Interestingly, members of the UK's immigrant lion community continue to utilise their first language and resist acquiring even the rudiments of English[8]. Zoo residents, however, speak, at best, a diluted version of Lionese, drawing on a much-reduced vocabulary. Inhabitants of safari parks display a broader range of articulations but this still represents a fraction of that which they employ in their native land.

Further information about Lionese may be found in the quarterly Journal of Leolinguistic Studies, of which Professor Sorenson is

Executive Academic Editor. Lionese is now offered as a module on a number of undergraduate Animal Studies degrees and although it is not yet available in the Teach Yourself series of books and downloads, the first certified intensive TLFL course is currently recruiting.

1   Sorenson, Ross—personal communication, 15th November 2013
2   The first Lionese-English dictionary is forthcoming from Dēor Press in 2016
3   'hffn', as used exclusively by the male lion
4   'hffngh', as used by lionesses
5   Sorenson, Ross (ed.) *Exit, Pursued by a Lion*, p. 862 (Warminster University Press, 2007)
6   Sorenson, Ross—personal communication, 22nd May 2014
7   Animal Languages of the World, p. 31 (Bestia Books, 2011)
8   Ibid., pp. 98-114

shamanic

summer drums
on the skin
of the sun

rattle of brassicas
and buddleia

segmented legs
bend
in new ways

enter inter-
stitial space

membrane
thin
as existence

from the place
that once was spine

now pimp
these wings—
get them inked

trim
with cath kidston fabric—

suck
with tongue
as nimble as a finger

this wonder
of unweight

crumpled memories
pump with blood
harden

Stage Four—Imago
the Life Cycle of the Large White

pupil pupates
into adult traveller
flitting to kuranda

antennae tingling for lingering
hints of fountaine

flashbacks fade
ragged
as cabbage

eclipsed by the wish
to dance the brimstone

ringlet   grizzled skipper
to fulfil the fritillary
fertility rite

trance music moves trans-
mute into flight

till sunbeat slows
wings dry and split
like honesty

comma
full stop

Zoomorphic

1.

The insomnia llama spits
in your mug of valerian tea.
When you try to mindfully breathe,
she chews bromegrass at your right ear,
regurgitating for hours
from stomachs one, two and three. She kicks
your counted sheep, hisses
at your downward dogs and twisting cobras.

From the occupied side of your bed,
she bids you pluck her double coat.
You card and spin a yawn of yarn,
weave exhausted scarves and shawls.
Your walls are restless
with hand-knit hangings, rugs toss
and turn on your floors.

Some nights, she drags you on a trek,
lugs all your frets in the pack on her back.
As you crawl across the high steppes,
the air thins your mind,
while a condor jabs your unsteady thighs.

Much later, once you've bathed
in clary sage and lavender,
her mate arrives.
His orgling while they copulate
would be quite soporific
if it only didn't augur
the birth of a herd.

2.

He doesn't need to swallow to feel it.
It's visible even from the outside now,
skulking in its den
when he awkwardly shaves in the morning.
Then, having stalked his vocal cords
and scent-marked his pharynx,
it emits, without warning,
when he opens his mouth to speak,
a freakish howl.

He wishes he could tame it, exchange it
for a lapdog that sees no reason to yap,
let it out each week on a leash of floss,
train it to sleep between his tonsils.

Better yet, trap it.
Lace Strepsils with strychnine.
Bribe his brother to shoot it for a trophy or its pelt.
Those who say *Let it stay—*
it belongs there—you'll soon get the benefit
are wrong. Oh, how he hates
this taste of wilderness claimed by an apex predator,
craves to build wheatfields from Lego again.

The beast in his throat is spoiling everything.
All the girls are laughing.
And it's giving him spots.

3.

In the cage between her legs, there lives a frigatebird.
Prevented from flexing its three-foot wings.
Pecking at the fingers that poke it through the bars.
Yoked to its pubic roost.
Feathers caked in dark.
And, despite the lack of space,
its bright red gular sac perpetually inflated.

She tight-squeezes her thighs.
Tugs her skirt hem past her knees.
Shifts from cheek to cheek on the two-seater settee.
Though she really should feed it pieces of marine iguana,
she wills herself to believe it isn't there.
Sit still. You're such a fidget, her mother sighs,
eyes never migrating from the TV.

Yet the frigatebird's eyes keep brimming
with sky — if the frigatebird were permitted
to fly, it would glide without
pause for weeks, tweaking fish from
shearwaters' beaks, seeking uplifts
to ride, thrilling never to reach the sides
of either air   or sea

Wovon die Tiere träumen, weiß ich nicht
— Sigmund Freud

**Is it the cheetah treads your dream,
or you who've entered its?**
— from 'The Cheetah' by Andrew Waterman

You're used to being dreamed by cows,
tugging subconscious udders,
recurrent as cud.

And you're used to being summoned by giraffes,
the sudden judder as you're called to walk small
in another spindly nap.

With koalas you relax into narrative,
and though it's taxing having to feature
for twenty hours each day,
it's less fatiguing than the months you once spent
tangled in the sleep of a hibernating bat.

You've learned that snakes' dreams are chaste
and literal—within them, you're a symbol
for nothing but yourself.
You've learned that geese never dream of flying,
while elephants recall every wrinkle of your role
and interpret you for weeks.

As for the cheetah, you're heaved into
her sleep just after she's eaten.
She's conjured you a gun
and though she strains to run away,
she's sprinting without moving.
And now you're made to prowl the plain.
And you're gaining on her.
Gaining. Gaining. Gaining.

Homophoca Vox Pop

I miss holding my breath.
I miss my status as a fallen angel.

My blubber hummed with old mariners' stories.
My flippers twitched with their tragedies,
with their occasional glory.

Here, I'm the woman
with the fingers that can't
tickle, can't
type, can't
hold a fork.
The woman who can only
talk dulse and bubbles.

≈

Hello! And a big warm Wednesday welcome to
tonight's show! We're gearing up for some *very*
special scenes, the first of their kind *ever* to
be shown live on national TV! We've got cameras
rigged up from *every* angle—right here on the
beach, up on the cliffs and even under water! We've
got camera traps! We've got rock-cams! We've got
kelp-cams! We've got infrared night vision cams!
Also joining us live is Megan from Seal With A
Kiss who's been analysing the data and predicting
exactly where the most incredible scenes of all
are going to be taking place. *Love* the t-shirt,
Megan! And we've also got Rick manning the heli-
cam, all set to bring you *spectacular* live footage
from the air! Rick, can you hear me?

≈

So now that he's back here,
a three-dimensional smear
on my designer recliner sofa,
what am I supposed to do?
Teach him some tricks? How to balance
my fury on his nose? How to leap
through the hoop of my disapproval?

Am I obliged to fall instantly back in love?
If he was more sun and private pool
than spume and rockslime
I might feel inclined to like him.

Will he expire without access to water?
I refuse to let him use
the jacuzzi bath or Petal Pink sink...

Deep breaths...Calm...Think...Think...

≈

Yes. We've, well, we've slightly revised
our assessment of the, uh, the gravity of the
situation and, well, as things currently stand,
I'd say that, yes, there is some small cause for
concern.

≈

Perhaps if I make it abundantly clear
there's no suitable water source here,
he'll haul himself away.
My alternative ploy will be to lure
him to the car with the Japanese koi
from the pond, then drive to some beach
and leave him.

≈

Well, uh, adolescent girls between the ages
of thirteen and seventeen seem to be the most
vulnerable...Yes, we must all be aware of the,
uh, warning signs. We must all be, uh, you know,
more vigilant.

≈

I was a quiet kid. Into nature.
Always down the beach after school
on my own.
Saw seals on loads of evenings.
Kept a detailed record.
Only May-the-fourth-eighty-eight's left blank.

≈

70

Yes, well, even though it'll mean redeploying funds from other critical areas of research, we're now looking into developing a vaccine...When? Well, at the, uh, well, at the earliest possible opportunity.

≈

What I saw that day wasn't beautiful.
She coughed up oil and water.
Spat plastic.
Fishing line was snagged in her hair.

But still, waves fell over themselves
in their eagerness to see.
Bivalves gaped on the tideline.
Marram grass stood on end
along the neck of the dunes.

For a lifetime, mist paused
in its forming.
For a moment, pebbles eroded
into sand.

≈

Journeys from sea to home are far from easy.
But they're a honk compared to the day
I found I could no longer part
my knees and thighs.

At first I feared I'd been converted to a mermaid,
but then hair and breasts got downsized
in favour of flab and fur. In the time
it took the tide to turn
I had to learn to untie
knots of wind, to steer
with new footflaps at the rear.
I had to earn the sea's esteem,
spurn the urge to scream
beneath its upchurned ceiling.

But oh, I miss the kindness of cushions,
the certainty of curtains and chairs.

Whenever I'm at my most scared, I surface
and feed on my silver-scaled memories
of being upright.

≈

I'm like duh! Haven't you guys noticed
something? Like some kinda pattern? Who's doing
the transforming here? Is it dudes in suits from
the corporate elite, all luxury SUVs and chi-
chi condos? You're fricking kidding, right? It's
women. Women who are sick to their waxed fannies
of working for crap pay and raising kids on their
own and scarfing down happy pills just so's they
can numb themselves to all the other dumb roles
that society says they gotta play. And now it's
like I can gain weight? I can get to hang out in
the sea all day? I can dive so deep I'll never be
found? Yeah, I'll have some of that.

≈

if she gets it from anyone
she gets it from her father
all I hope is it's a phase
she's going through
it's her father's fault
you mark my words
his side of the family
always was a bit odd
all I hope
is it's a phase
she's going through
as for gorging cod all day
just think of the smell
it's no wonder I'm on tablets
for my nerves

≈

I miss the tidal chat—
all those blabs of bladderwrack
that probe the high water line
for bottles with desperate messages inside,
then gossip with clots of Irish moss
about what they find.

≈

Come back with me, he says!
Is he honestly suggesting
I must make the rash
and, quite frankly, melodramatic choice
to be more aquatic?
That I should give up this house, the car, my clothes
for a shapeless grey skin?
That I must ruin my hair? These nails?

Wouldn't it be more fair
for him to give up the sea?

Here, after all, he's free of sealers. And killer whales.
And he at least still seems to have a vague appreciation
of hors d'oeuvres and cocktails.

And, in time, again, quite possibly, me.

≈

Her. Again. Quite possibly.
A life free of sealers.
A life free of sea.

A life of concealing webbed fingers
in sewn-up sleeves,
of periwinkles clinging
to wrinkled pink cheeks.

Her. In time. Quite possibly.
A life free of sealers.
A life free of sea.

A life without flippering up
storms, without breathing forth
fog, without flipping over
the boats of those whose hunt
for mammalblood's a frivolous sport.

≈

Will populations of this elusive mammal
hybrid increase and stabilise? Hard to say. As
I've consistently advocated, we need to invest
heavily in a captive breeding programme to ensure
its long-term survival.

≈

I've done my bit for myth,
added to the yawp of yarns, sloughed off
my skin and danced
for lovestruck fishermen.

Sick of them, I've risked more northern waters,
quivered in my lair
as the ghost bear creaked the ice overhead, fled
guns and clubs, bled tears for the cubs
culled for fur for hoods and purses.

≈

In the meantime, I understand there's a
Twitter-driven taxonomy competition with online
voting that will lead to the adoption of an official
new species name.

≈

I eventually gave in
and made room for his skin
in my walk-in wardrobe.
Can't you hear, he kept saying,
my sealskin sigh?

No, I'd reply. *That's just the whine
of the DVD player on standby.*

≈

Touch it, I'd tell her.
Feel the lining of regret.
Feel the outer hairs pining
for gutweed and maerl beds.

≈

There's only one thing to do and that's hide
their bloody skins——that's how it was done in the
old days and no-one came to any harm. It may have
taken them a while to get used to living on dry
land again but we all have to do things we don't
want to in life.

≈

I made her promise
not to lock it in her closet
and swallow the key.
I made her promise not to disrobe,
to try it on over her own clothes, please.

≈

Never mind all the bloody do-gooders saying
'Leave them be, they're only expressing themselves
and who are you to decide what's normal?' If God
had wanted us to turn into seals, He'd have given
us *all* flippers and fins.

≈

The memory's sharp as a gannet's beak.
When I tried it on I suddenly believed
I could speak shrimp and brine.
It made me feel oceanic.
Made me high as a spring tide.

≈

It was monstrously big for her.
Wrinkled. Looked ridiculous.

≈

Never mind the size!
I can shrink it! Take it in!
Trim the sleeves to fit my arms!
Repurpose your fins!

≈

    Gaia is wounded and thereby we are wounded
too. Her trees weep red sap. She wheezes with
coal-fired pollution. We've maimed her, raped her,
laid waste to the curves of her hills and dales.
Why, then, should we be so surprised when nature-
deprived souls turn seal to effect a reconnection?

≈

all I hope is it's a phase she's going through

≈

When she said
I've got something special to tell you
and I've brought you
to my special place,

when she said
we've been together
six-months-two-weeks-and-three-days now
so it feels like it's time,

when she said
you wait here on the beach for a sec,
I'll go back to the hut.
Soon as I'm ready
I'll call,

I thought, new tattoo?
Nipple ring?
Whatever, my luck's in.

≈

if she gets it from anyone
she gets it from her father

≈

@newspeciesname   sealman   manseal   phoca
sapiens   sealoid   sealus domesticus   homophoca
Sammy #selkiecomp

≈

it's no wonder I'm on tablets
for my nerves

≈

It was last October.
Some photographer-bloke,
full-stretch on the sand,
big sodding lens thrust
at a new-born pup.

Then, suddenly, shouting—
couldn't get up,
couldn't grip his camera.
Fleece and jeans upheaving
with blubber. Yell swelling
into bark and grunt.

≈

We've got rock-cams! We've got kelp-cams!
We've got infrared night vision cams!

≈

My thoughts, caught
out of their element,
could only hump along.
Flinched at his skin,
marbled like a counter top.
Blinked at the lump of him.
Like a thumping great slug.

Herring gulls heckled.
Whelk shells echoed
with speedboats.
The tide turned
its back.

≈

It's all the foreigners coming over that's
the problem—taking our jobs, overrunning our
towns. I'm not a bit surprised there's some of us
deciding we'd rather go off and live in the sea.

≈

Maybe if I hadn't said
Christ, how'd you get
that thing in here?
Jess, where you hiding?
This is a joke, yeah?
What the—?

Maybe if I hadn't done a runner,
legged it to the dunes,
trying not to throw up.

Maybe if I hadn't waited
four-hours-twelve-minutes-thirty-eight-seconds
to go back to the hut.

≈

Yes, in the end, he went back.
Without me.
But lick my lips
and I can still taste him—
salty with promise.

≈

Found her flipflops
tank top phone
by the bottled gas.
Found lipgloss fags
handfuls of hair.
Found that hot pair
of cut-offs.

≈

Whatever the cause—and some are, rather
implausibly, interpreting it as a repressed desire
to return to the maternal womb—we can no longer
view these cases as isolated outbreaks.

≈

Her old man thinks I'm scum,
won't come near me,
swears she's been abducted —
won't hear me when I try to tell him
otherwise.
He's got the cops on the case
country-wide.

≈

Thanks to the ubiquity of the internet, the
symptoms are proving impossible to contain.

≈

Before me and Jess met,
the only things I made
were dinner for one,
passionless love,
a fuss.

But now I'm sewing a skin,
stitching flippers and fins.
Know what? I'm growing up.

≈

He leaves me limpets
and glimmers
of fish on the shore each night.

The Bermuda Blue carpet still retains
the shape of him.
The sofa leather's rucked
into seven waves
and I never want to make it flat.

≈

In fact, we currently seem to be witnessing a
rash of copycat transformations that could rapidly
escalate into a pandemic.

≈

Can guess what her old man's thinking—
'Quit the Icarus shit
and help me find my daughter.'

Well, get this—
I'm swimming twice a day,
both down the pool
and in open water.
I've learnt to free-dive
and I'm piling on weight,
chugging down
loads of protein shakes.

≈

However, let's be absolutely clear about
this.

≈

Gubfobs blasherbip, flib

≈

There are no immediate plans—

≈

gubfobs shrull glupper.

≈

I repeat, no immediate plans—

≈

That's sealspeak for 'I miss you, babe—

≈

to initiate a cull.

≈

I'm on my way.'

Either stop writing, or write like a rat.

If the writer is a sorcerer, it is because writing is a becoming, writing is traversed by strange becomings that are not becomings-writer but becomings-rat, becomings-insect, becomings-wolf, etc.
— from *A Thousand Plateaus* by Gilles Deleuze and Félix Guattari

1.

Never more than six feet away from one, it's said.
Yet it's not enough to cultivate a tail

and to fail to cut your nails. You must
be able to make people pale and recoil

in shock at your endurance. You must root
through shredded synonyms and stewed piles

of similes. You must prove you can chew through
chicken wire and vile reviews. Yes,

there will be days of mazes and races
you don't want to run and times when you'll abide

by the Pied Piper of perfect rhymes,
when you're injected with the virus of effecting

what others require. But there will also come a time
when critics will smell you with zest, not suspicion,

as you scratch your own route through Hamelin.

2.

you're   wall-wise
     waiting
           to learn   what's said
    poised   to pilfer
                    turns-of-phrase
     and   quirks of
                   character   then
                quickshift
   to   the next
               vertical   surface
 where   you filch
       more   overheards
    then   work   to clear
          the blur
       from   your
           compound   eyes
as the   speedofwhatyousee
    is confounding
                  howyouwrite
    and   wow
       you've   mastered
    flight
           no spine
     six legs   and
  an   ovipositor
   and   yet
        you   can't
    quite   seem
      to   insect   yourself
completely
     can't   face
     feasting
   on   fruitrot
    and   faeces
        in   spite   of
    the   current   buzz
       for   fictional
death   and
           disease

3.

Today, you're glutted with grandmothers and rocks.
The big eyes you have are blind to binding deadlines.
And you're constrained by a chain made of *sorry... unsuitable...*
doesn't meet our publication needs at this time.

But once the shackles snap, you'll guzzle
the sunrise, huff and puff and blow
           those deadlines
                down,
then suckle, on your thickly-worded slopes,
one lucky child.

Witch Fulfilment

The wand is only for show.
What matters is that I'm herb-perfect—
choosing the leaves that no-one else knows,
using them before they're swapped
for monocultural crops
or holiday apartment blocks,
before the sea slops over my island's edges.

What matters is that I've picked the least loved beast—
the one whose head gets plonked on a platter,
an apple stopping its gob;
the one whose first name is fascist;
the one who's said to gush sweat
yet has no waste glands;
the one who's crammed with cash, then sacrificed.

What matters is that casting churls into swine
is the finest alliance of science and art.
Reworking skin (fleshy and pink
like posh peers) and heart
(porcine valves routinely heal humans)
is the easy part. It's trotters and snout
that spark self-doubt and dread of failing.

What matters is that I relish
the finishing touch (the tail-twirl flourish)
and can't wait to translate when the grunts of the litter
curse me *(Circe, quit your sodding sorcery…*
Circery…you menopausal bitch…) As they lurch
from quaffing herbs to loss of words
I, too, am changed.

Nereid

1.

The sensation caught me by surprise—
a sickle fin seeking to breach my spine
and the notion that sea-nymphing no longer satisfied.
Then   *click*   I found my new form by sound—
for a moment *click click* I was both dolphin and rider
then wholly *clickclickclick* the creature whose back
I'd sat astride.

>   Pleasure pods!
>   Bottlenosed joy!

I felt me vibrate with such echo-elation
that only the threat of nylon nets
          could unself me.

2.

When the urge returned, she yearned
     for land—to pugmark mud, stalk

on all fours, roar as her fur performed
     its striping. Yet each time she tigers now,

it's more tiring than before, as she hunts
     not just for prey but for pungent signs

that her kind has stopped declining.

3.

Next—ditch
backbone. Chill
blood. Don't
just itch
        to switch
to a glamour-mammal.
Meet Thetis the Remix—
inveterate invertebrate.
Stag beetle rootling
for putrid fruit
and sap, all set
to raise
        its mandibles
and fight
                for what remains
    of its habitat.

4.

Now roots shoot from soles; your torso's rigid. Leaves unfurl
from each twigit. You do little but
breathe   breathe   breathe,
then lead a meditation on the miracle of medicine in trees.
You'd shapestay in this way for growth-rings galore,
if it wasn't that your forest floor quakes
with that felling
                                    feeling.

5.

These days, when I crave to change, there are fewer forms to choose
from. Gone is the time when I could think 'corncrake' and a reflex
crex would swell my throat, when I could come over all iguana and
sense my neck blue-cresting. And as my skull births twin horns
and I bulge to megafauna, I can't decide if I'm the last in the line.
Or the Western Black Rhino in the savannah of the mind.

Silvertip

She loves how honey drizzles
and stickies his fur
as he plods to the bus stop
and how shopping now means forage
for tubers, forbs, roots
and nuts of the whitebark pine.

She hates her workmates' porridge-gossip,
her mother's warning horns and wails
that the pigtailed girl who always learnt her German verbs
should come to this.

She hikes through his taiga mind,
defies his bluff charges,
sings *I've Got You Under My Skin* at blind corners
and shifts her desk upwind of him,
thrilled he still scents her
even when streets away.

She chucks out her ladyshave,
checks belly, back, breasts
for silvertipped flecks of hair,
takes care to ingest twenty thousand calories each day.
For she means to wintersleep with him,
deeper than any princess-threat,
in the den of his boreal breath.

She will lick what she births
into a mix of huffs and words, then emerge
in spring, as mother
of the ancestors of a new race.

Appendix

Instructions For Use
(English version)

(i)

Your new tawny owl
has 256 MB of memory.

To learn the important basics,
browse the Welcome
To Your Tawny Owl booklet
that came with your tawny owl.

Switching from another owl?
Open the tawny owl help menu
and see the New To Tawny Owl section.
It will help you use
your previous owl knowledge
to get started on a tawny.

If your tawny owl fails
to start, see Problems That Prevent You
From Using Your Tawny Owl
at the end of this guide.

Because your tawny owl is so light,
you can take it with you to the office,
library, school or wherever
you work and play.

The main thing you gain
by using a tawny owl
is stability.
You and your tawny owl
may go for years
without witnessing
a crash.

(ii)

Red squirrel is hygienic, efficient and safe. Dual action
for effective degreasing. Kind and gentle to your hands.

No need to keep red squirrel out of reach
of children or use in a well-ventilated area.

Red squirrel has minimum impact on aquatic life
and is also suitable for septic tanks.

Always read the label. One squeeze is enough.

(iii)

Hardy perennial.
Average contents
84 seeds.

Sow pipistrelles
2 cm (1 in) deep
from March to July

in a weed-free site
that has been raked
to a fine tilth.

WATER THOROUGHLY
and keep watered
until established.

When large enough to handle,
thin your pipistrelles
to 8 cm (3 in) apart.

Pipistrelles can also be sown
indoors or under cloches
for an early crop.

Pipistrellus pipistrellus
is a fast-growing pipistrelle variety
for continuous sowing.

Ideal for the edges
of borders
or for creating

a permanent
ornamental bed.
Always remove

spent pipistrelle heads
to encourage
further blooming.

(iv)

It's never too late to create great skin!
Reduce the signs of ageing
and tighten your skin with Water Vole!
For smooth, young-looking skin, massage
Water Vole gently but thoroughly
into your face and neck morning and evening.
Our luxury Water Vole is the only
intensive anti-ageing treatment on the market
that boosts the skin's vital functions.

A unique formula for a visibly youthful look,
Water Vole contains an exclusive technology
that stimulates the elastin support network
of the skin, improving firmness and bounce-back.
For optimal results, use Water Vole
with our age-defying Bank Vole,
and Pygmy Shrew from our anti-wrinkle range.

Water Vole is the best product
I've ever used! Within a week,
I could see and feel the difference! —
Miss S. Arvicola, Tewksbury

Water Vole — the professionals' choice!